476 Quick & Practical

D0868023

TOPICS

COMMUNICATING SUCCESSFULLY

Customers form their impressions of an organization from the way they are treated — and from the way that organization's employees treat one another. Here are some ways to impress your customers and co-workers.

When You Talk

• **Project your** sincerity. Strong belief, enthusiasm, energy — these are the qualities that cause your listeners to lean forward to hear what you are saying.

• **Avoid arguing.** Most people tend to defend their positions with strong rebuttals. If you want to convince someone that your view is the right one, start by emphasizing points of agreement. Then try to get the other person to accept several minor points that lead logically to your major position.

• **Teach yourself** not to interrupt when talking on the phone. What the other person is saying should be more important to you than what you will say — especially when the person is talking. Teach yourself to pause for two seconds after the person finishes his or her statement. The pause, according to *The Telephone Selling Report,* communicates that you are listening so you can understand the person's needs better.

© Briefings Publishing Group, a Division of Douglas Publications LLC
2807 North Parham Road, Suite 200, Richmond, VA 23294
(800)722-9221 • (703)518-2343 outside the U.S.
Fax: (703)684-2136

Getting Others to Agree

Persuading others often depends on getting them to identify with a problem, idea or suggestion. Communication expert Earl Newsom identifies these four persuasion principles:

• **Familiarity and Trust.** People accept ideas from people and organizations they trust. *Suggestion:* Use a speaker the audience knows or cite an experience the reader shares and accepts.

• **Identification.** People accept opinions or points of view when they can see some direct effect on their ambitions. Cite audience benefits rather than your purpose.

• **Clarity.** People accept clearly expressed ideas. Avoid jargon and messages that lack a clear motive and organization.

• **Action.** People accept ideas when they are accompanied by a convenient action plan to carry out the ideas. Show *how* you propose to make a difference with your ideas rather than just announcing you're for change.

Other tips:

• **Research reported** in the *Journal of Nonverbal Behavior* suggests you should increase your eye contact when speaking and reduce it when listening — if you want to be seen as more powerful.

• **When talking** to two or more people, don't sit between them. It's hard to maintain eye contact when you do.

Earning Respect for Your Ideas

When you have an idea, proposal or opinion, and you want others to agree, try these tips:

• **Be interesting.** If you aren't, whatever is being said won't be listened to.

• **Be personal.** It must appeal to the self-interests of others.

• **Be easy to** understand. If your idea isn't seen as workable, then it won't be accepted.

Working With Others

Consider these tips when communicating with colleagues:

• **Ask a** close colleague to tell you if you're overusing any words or phrases. *Example:* The phrase *by and large.* If you are, others might spend time counting the number of times you use the word or expression in a presentation rather than listening to what you're saying.

• **Learn the** names of as many people in other departments as possible. People are impressed by — and remember the names of — people who call them by name.

• **To befriend** colleagues and build trust for you and your department, show others how *your* work can help get *their* work done faster or better. *Example:* If your weekly summaries contain data that would be valuable to others, offer to place these people on the routing list. *Goal:* Convince others that what you do helps them.

• **Learn to** write one- or two-paragraph notes of thanks to people who help you. It's a classy thing to do.

• **Smile.** People who smile are perceived to be more intelligent than people who don't.

• **Everybody wants** people around who work hard and get the job done. Gain that reputation by doing those things that the boss asks for and by communicating as succinctly and thoroughly as possible with others.

• **Don't spend** a lot of time on things that aren't important just because you're good at those activities. People who get ahead establish priorities and designate time to work on them.

• **Don't "bad-mouth"** anyone. You never know who is related to someone or who knows someone personally as well as professionally. That someone might be important to you someday.

• **Learn to** take prudent risks and generate ideas that will increase profits. Know when to be impatient with busy bosses to be sure key projects are moving along properly. *Also:* Remind bosses of new ideas that may be lost on the bottom of a pile. Most bosses appreciate gentle prods that help keep them on target.

• **Learn to** make effective presentations. If you're not a good speaker, then become one.

• **Be polite.** Use "Please" and "Thank you." It's a simple thing to do, but too many people forget to do so. If someone does you a favor, be sure to follow up with a "Thank you."

• **Make yourself** a comfortable person to be around. Everyone enjoys working with nice people.

© Briefings Publishing Group, a Division of Douglas Publications LLC
2807 North Parham Road, Suite 200, Richmond, VA 23294
(800)722-9221 • (703)518-2343 outside the U.S.
Fax: (703)684-2136

BUILDING TEAMWORK

Team members need to know how to get along in good and bad times. They need to know how to show — and get — the kind of respect and cooperation that makes things happen.

Here are some suggestions to help you and your organization build strong work teams to get ahead and succeed.

Working as a Team Member

To build teamwork:

• **Promise only** what you intend to deliver — even if it means you have to say "no" to protect your reputation of dependability.

• **Deliver what** you promise — and more — on time.

• **Keep confidences** and resist the urge to use private information to appear valuable, important or popular to colleagues.

• **Stay on** top of the information flow in your field. *Remember:* The strongest person at the meeting is the one with information and the ability to use it to persuade others.

• **Use a** sense of humor to keep serious situations from becoming unmanageable and minor situations from becoming problems.

• **Know how** to congratulate and motivate others.

• **Be fair** in discussions. Avoid power cliques, extreme positions and personal attacks.

• **Know the** organization's business, history, mores and codes of behavior — and follow them.

• **Smile.** It's difficult to get angry with someone who's genuinely happy.

Speak Positively to Others

We feel positive about our jobs when we receive compliments for our work, when others ask our advice and when people simply know and use our names. Use these tips to get along:

• **Cite specific** activities. Say, "I appreciate the time and effort you put in on the ABC proposal," rather than, "Good job."

• **Use the** person's name. Link the name to something positive. Say, "Pat, thanks for coming in early to organize the meeting," rather than, "Thanks for

coming in to organize the meeting."
- **Use a** standard. Say, "Mary, your report looks like an award-winner."
- **Recognize complimentors.** Say, "Thanks, Bob, for noticing. You've made my day." *Caution:* Don't return a compliment after you've received one. It probably diminishes the value of the first compliment.
- **Ask people's** advice or opinion. Say, "Jennifer, what do you think of the plan?" or, "We haven't heard from Jennifer yet. I'd like her ideas on this."

How to Cope With Criticism
- **Be honest** with yourself. Nobody's perfect. You probably have faults like the rest of your colleagues.
- **Reverse roles** with the critic. If you were in the place of the other person, would you be saying the same things?
- **Get disagreements** in the open. If you don't agree with the criticism, tell the critic. Don't harbor resentment.
- **Don't complain** during the criticism. Listen to the comments. *Reason:* You'll appear more mature.
- **Control your** emotions. If you feel stressed during the criticism, look at the criticism technically, not personally.
- **Disarm your** critic. Your first response should be, "How could I have done better?" The answer may tell you what norm was expected.
- **Change your** behavior. Use the criticism as a guide to change. Later, draw the critic's attention to the change you've made.

How to Criticize Others
To criticize properly, be helpful to others.
- **Use "I,"** not "You" statements. Admit to your frustration.
- **Do it** privately.
- **Fault the** action, the behavior or the ideas — not the person.
- **Conclude with** support for the worker, rather than with verbal abuse. Encouragement pays off.

How to Resolve an Argument
- **Listen to** the other person without interrupting. You'll get your chance, and a better one, if you first give the other person your uninterrupted attention.

• **Pause before** responding. If you answer too quickly, you send the signal that you haven't heard, or don't care about, what the other person is saying.

• **State your** position calmly and logically. Use evidence, not opinion.

• **Use a** third person. Sometimes an arbiter can remove the emotion generated by disagreements.

• **Let your** opponent save face. Offer the other person a way to come over to your side. Say, "I understand why you felt that way before you received this new information."

How to Cope With Angry Colleagues

• **Don't show** your anger. You can do it nonverbally, too, so beware. If both boss and worker are angry, solutions become even more difficult.

• **Never talk** down to an angry person. Don't patronize the person with statements such as, "You're upset now, so why don't you calm down and we'll continue when you're more rational."

• **Avoid threats.** Anger is a heightened state of self-defense. Threats only make the person more defensive and more angry.

How to Accept an Apology

When you accept an apology, don't gloat or embarrass the other person. Say, "I accept and appreciate your apology." Or, "I accept your apology, but I want you to know that I too contributed to the problem and apologize for doing so." As you accept the apology, smile and extend your hand.

Other Tips

• **Offer to** help co-workers when you've finished your work. They may reciprocate when you need help.

• **If you** make a serious mistake, be the first to tell your boss. Don't let someone who dislikes you be the first to share the information.

• **Ask your** boss for direction on an assignment and for clarification if needed. Don't guess. *Remember:* If the boss thinks it's important, it's important.

• **Don't be** a constant complainer. No one likes a whiner. If you have suggestions to remedy a problem, share them with the right person.

• **When your** boss says your help is needed immediately, get right on it.

• **Strive for** excellence. Don't tolerate foolish mistakes, or anything that

© Briefings Publishing Group, a Division of Douglas Publications LLC
2807 North Parham Road, Suite 200, Richmond, VA 23294
(800)722-9221 • (703)518-2343 outside the U.S.
Fax: (703)684-2136

communicates that you're not a quality person.
- **If you** must present bad news to a boss or colleague, accompany it with a suggested solution to the problem.
- **Be enthusiastic** about your work. People like "alive" colleagues. Don't overdo it, however.
- **Share the** credit when you're successful but be quick to take the blame if something goes wrong in your area of responsibility.
- **Ask for** information you need instead of grumbling about being uninformed.
- **Don't be** a Monday morning quarterback. Your after-the-fact negative comments will hurt others. Limit your remarks to comments that can change things or avoid problems.
- **Make your** boss look good. When the boss is promoted, there's a chance something good will happen to you.
- **Work hard.** This advice might seem old-fashioned but hard workers are valued by just about everyone.

HANDLING CONFLICT

Don't let workplace conflict interfere with your ability to enjoy your job. Use the ideas and suggestions here to make sure you know how to use conflict as a catalyst for innovation and success.

Why Conflict Occurs

True office fighting and bickering usually result only when people aren't managing conflict well. Generally, emotional outbursts in the workplace occur during conflict when:
- **People feel** as if their individual needs or opinions are being ignored in discussions.
- **The real** issues in a conflict have been obscured by minor issues that may be only indirectly related to the actual issue causing the conflict.
- **A workplace** environment exists that discourages people from openly discussing their true feelings about workplace issues.

© Briefings Publishing Group, a Division of Douglas Publications LLC
2807 North Parham Road, Suite 200, Richmond, VA 23294
(800)722-9221 • (703)518-2343 outside the U.S.
Fax: (703)684-2136

Careful Listening Is One Key

Your listening skills play a vital role in managing conflict overall. *Some tips:*

• **Interrupt only** to clarify a point, not to make a point. Let your actions communicate that you always are carefully listening to others' viewpoints and that your responses consider others' viewpoints. Don't get hung up on winning minor points during an exchange. Focus on the major issue causing the conflict.

• **Don't respond** too quickly. Poor listeners often are formulating a response in their own minds before another person has finished talking. Good listeners concentrate on the point the speaker is trying to make — and wait a moment before responding. Give yourself time to reflect on what you just heard and to formulate your response.

Keep Your Emotions in Check

Emotions generally are the catalysts that cause conflict management to degenerate into office warfare — and a situation that may produce a few short-term winners but many long-term losers. *Some tips:*

• **Stay calm.** Be assertive but not aggressive. Conflict advances to dangerous bickering when emotions overtake clear thinking on issues. To avoid this problem, stick to relevant facts when expressing your own thoughts. Never try to force a resolution with threats or demands.

• **Don't fear** involving others in the conflict if they can add an objective point of view. Sometimes people too close to a problem can lose sight of the real issue. *Result:* Emotions and preconceived ideas interfere with their abilities to seek a solution. Often, outsiders with no emotional attachment to an issue can help everyone involved to return to the real issue at hand.

• **Be a** gracious winner and loser. Ideally, of course, successfully managing conflict means that everyone wins. But even if you finally can admit to yourself that your original viewpoint may have been wrong, you may have a tough time admitting it to others.

The solution: Remember that successful conflict management provides results that are good for the organization as a whole and, therefore, good for everyone in the organization. Take satisfaction in your role in helping to resolve a conflict, no matter how closely the final outcome resembles your original viewpoint.

© Briefings Publishing Group, a Division of Douglas Publications LLC
2807 North Parham Road, Suite 200, Richmond, VA 23294
(800)722-9221 • (703)518-2343 outside the U.S.
Fax: (703)684-2136

• **Always keep** an open mind. Don't go into any conflict with your mind made up.

• **Focus on** finding solutions — not on winning. Winning debates may temporarily give your ego a boost, but does little to resolve conflicts.

Focus on the Future

Don't fall victim to the natural temptation to dredge up past complaints in current conflicts. *Also:*

• **Resist the** urge to affix blame. Solve the problem first. Then, look for the cause — to prevent the problem from surfacing again.

• **Get agreement** on the precise problem to be resolved. Write it down if necessary so that everyone agrees on exactly what the problem is.

• **Keep discussions** focused on specific goals. Don't let debates wander into unrelated issues. Keep reminding participants of the specific problem under consideration.

Your Public Role

Being able to communicate clearly and impartially is a skill that few people get formal training in before being asked to do it.

Consider: You're in a crowded meeting with your boss and co-workers, as well as managers and employees from other parts of the company. As an issue is being debated, you agree with some points and disagree with others. At times, you even disagree with your boss. The meeting leader looks at you and asks, "What do you think?"

Here are some suggestions on how to handle the situation:

• **Make it** clear in your response that you understand the situation and want to continue helping to find a solution that will benefit everyone.

• **Be careful** to support persons in authority — including, of course, your own boss. But feel free to express a different viewpoint on issues that won't directly challenge anyone's specific authority. If you have a strong disagreement in an area of authority, save that concern and express it privately to your boss later.

It's an Ongoing Process

Just as you don't want to affix blame or claim credit when an issue is

© Briefings Publishing Group, a Division of Douglas Publications LLC
2807 North Parham Road, Suite 200, Richmond, VA 23294
(800)722-9221 • (703)518-2343 outside the U.S.
Fax: (703)684-2136

resolved, you also don't want to fall into the trap of believing that conflicts are resolved for good.

Some conflicts will be present all the time and will demand ongoing management. *The result:* You should be working toward the day when everyone possesses the skills needed to manage conflict successfully.

DEALING WITH DIFFICULT PEOPLE

Each of us has to deal with some people who make our jobs difficult. Use the tips and techniques here to find out how to handle them.

Don't Take It Personally

Don't get too upset when someone verbally attacks you or your organization. Chances are the person doesn't mean anything personal.

It's not unreasonable, of course, to react personally when confronted.

To overcome this type of response, you simply have to learn that you're probably the target because you're the unlucky person who happened to be there when the complainer decided to let loose.

Some tips when you're the target:

• **Offer a** quick apology. "We're sorry, this shouldn't have happened ..." will go a long way toward soothing an upset customer or client.

Remember: You should apologize on behalf of the organization — even if your actions had nothing to do with creating the problem.

Later you can sort out who in the organization could have handled this situation better to begin with. Right now your job is to represent the organization well and work to fix the problem before it gets any worse.

• **Express your** concern and empathy as the person describes the problem. By showing your concern, you show that you care. A statement such as, "You must have felt terrible when you received a past-due notice after paying us on time a month ago," helps the person feel as if you know what she or he is feeling.

• **Move promptly** to fix whatever the problem is. People get most upset when they feel powerless against an organization. You can restore the person's "power" by simply making the person feel as if he or she has found the right person to solve the problem.

One method: Explain to the person just what you plan to do next and when the situation will be resolved.

• **Act on** your promises right away. If you can't resolve a problem while the person waits, put the process in motion immediately to solve the probler Follow up internally to make sure that others who may get involved do their part to fix the problem promptly. A difficult person will become almost impossible to deal with if he or she has to make a return visit to complain — especially after you had promised to fix the problem.

• **Suggest changes** in your job or policies that may help you or others in the organization handle problems. If an invoice change requires a manager's signature, and the manager isn't always available, perhaps someone else on the staff can be given this responsibility too. Making people wait, while problems they didn't even create are fixed, just makes bad customer relations worse.

• **Always follow** up. Even if a customer leaves satisfied, it's important that you call a day or two later to make sure that the person is still satisfied with the outcome.

I'm So Angry I Could...

Facing someone's anger can be a frightening ordeal. *To do your best:*

• **Recognize a** person's anger and treat it seriously. Using humor to try to overcome someone's anger is rarely a good idea. An upset person usually isn't in a joking mood. And your attempt to lighten the situation will almost certainly make things worse.

• **Listen carefully.** The best way to acknowledge someone's anger is to show that you share the concern and are willing to take the time to learn about the problem that has created the anger. Respond in ways that demonstrate your concern. *Example:* "I'm not surprised that you're upset. You should expect finished reports when everyone knew what the deadline was."

• **Take your** time. No matter how much other pressure you're under, it's important to take the time needed to deal with an upset person. By making an angry person feel rushed, you may make him or her feel as if you have more pressing concerns to deal with.

Important: Many angry people become much easier to deal with once they've simply had the chance to express their anger. Don't rush this process. Let them have their say. Then go about trying to fix their concerns.

© Briefings Publishing Group, a Division of Douglas Publications LLC
2807 North Parham Road, Suite 200, Richmond, VA 23294
(800)722-9221 • (703)518-2343 outside the U.S.
Fax: (703)684-2136

• **Don't monopolize** the conversation. Angry people think they know exactly what went wrong to create their anger. Although they may embellish a detail or two, they usually are right, for the most part. Because of this, they also are the ideal people to suggest an appropriate solution. Try to get them to tell you what they think should be done as a result of whatever they're complaining about.

I'm Right. That's It.

Irrational statements and demands often result when someone is acting out internal impulses or feelings that may have little to do with the situation causing the problem.

You don't have to agree with the person's position — but it often helps to express understanding for his or her point of view. By doing this, you may be able to uncover the real reasons behind the complaint as you continue your conversation with the person.

Why this is important: It may be difficult to persuade such a person with logical arguments alone. You must uncover the real reasons behind the arguments.

Dealing One-on-One

Why is it that our best arguments and remarks seem to come to us well after confrontations have ended? *One reason:* The emotions that accompany confrontations often interfere with our otherwise well-developed conversational skills.

To guide yourself in confrontational conversations:

• **Try to** keep the conversation focused on the facts of the situation. Avoid any temptation to try to guess at facts or figures. Your credibility will be destroyed. Few people want to deal with others who aren't seriously in command of the facts.

• **Stay away** from absolute pronouncements or demands. *Reason:* Absolute statements almost always guarantee more confrontation and less conversation. By qualifying your comments, you soften them and invite a response that may help you to find common ground with a complaining person.

Examples:

Absolute — "We have a 30-day, money-back policy that expired for you a week ago. Sorry, that's our policy."

Qualified — "We do limit our refunds to 30 days after purchase. But we don't want any unsatisfied customers. Tell me what you'd consider fair at this point and I'll see if there is something I can do to help you."

It's Not You...

Beware when people say, "It's nothing personal, but ..." Sometimes what follows is indeed personal.

If you believe someone's complaint with you is based on something personal, ask yourself:

• **Am I** missing some hidden agenda? Do I threaten this person in some way — even if it isn't my fault? Is the person trying to boost his or her personal power or standing, perhaps at my expense?

• **How can I** take responsibility for forging a solution? *Tip:* Look for no-lose solutions where each of you can benefit. *One way:* Try to find objectives or priorities you both share.

Important: Try to foster an atmosphere in your office that communicates that it's best to confront problems and concerns as soon as they surface.

Try to:

• **Resist the** urge to give someone the silent treatment. No matter how offensive or unfair someone's comments or charges may have been, keeping quiet will only make things worse. Your hurt feelings — and those of the other person's — will fester. And your relationship will continue to worsen.

• **Avoid ongoing** feuds. *Why:* Productivity in your workplace will suffer. People will waste time worrying about how to discuss things with you and the person you're feuding with, how to avoid any appearance of playing favorites when dealing with each of you and how to keep you apart. *Results:* Other staffers will grow frustrated — and supervisors will grow annoyed.

SATISFYING CUSTOMERS

The tips and ideas in this section will help you deal with customers and keep them happy.

© Briefings Publishing Group, a Division of Douglas Publications LLC
2807 North Parham Road, Suite 200, Richmond, VA 23294
(800)722-9221 • (703)518-2343 outside the U.S.
Fax: (703)684-2136

What May We Do for You?

To give customers the best care possible:

• **Help customers** who are in a hurry by placing large signs, giving them instructions or directions, where they can see them.

• **Know the** names of your company's most important customers. When they call with problems or requests, give their needs top priority.

• **Never say,** "We can't help you." Instead, help customers by finding other sources to meet their needs. You'll score points with them and they'll be back for those things you can do for them.

• **Many customers** show up or call during their lunch hour and need your services. Make sure that lunch breaks are arranged so that there's ample coverage between noon and one o'clock.

• **If you're** unable to serve customers because you must do something else, try to perform those duties where customers can't see you. Otherwise, they'll think you're ignoring them when actually you're not even available to them.

• **Ask customers** for suggestions. When you do, you communicate that their opinions count and that you want to do what's needed to keep them as customers.

• **Come up** with options for your customers. Show them several ways to meet a goal or solve a problem. Discuss each option, but let the customer make the decision.

How Do We Look?

Your body language and the appearance of your work space can tell customers more than your words. Remember to:

• **Look directly** at the customer and smile broadly. Peering at a customer over your glasses may create the impression that you think you're superior. Folding your arms may imply a lack of openness. Sloppy posture can lead a customer to think you're bored.

• **Keep your** work space somewhere between clean and messy to make people feel welcome. A lot of clutter may give customers the feeling that they're intruding or interrupting you. When nothing's out of place, they may see you as rigid and unfriendly. Plants or posters can make visitors feel more comfortable, according to the Administrative Management Society.

• **Arrange your** work area so that you're facing the space where customers enter. There'll be less chance of your failing to see a customer who's just come in.

© Briefings Publishing Group, a Division of Douglas Publications LLC
2807 North Parham Road, Suite 200, Richmond, VA 23294
(800)722-9221 • (703)518-2343 outside the U.S.
Fax: (703)684-2136

Listening Pays Off

Listening is as important as talking. Be patient, ask customers follow-up questions and go over their statements. *To listen well:*

• **Give customers** your undivided attention. If you don't, you're telling them that you're bored or uninterested. Don't let your eyes wander and don't keep on working at your desk. Don't take phone calls or let your co-workers interrupt you. If you really must be interrupted, get the customer's approval first.

• **Avoid doodling** or fidgeting while a customer is speaking. These actions communicate that you aren't interested in the speaker's problem or request.

• **Paraphrase what** the speaker has said to you to be certain you heard and understood correctly. *Example:* "To make sure I understand this, we normally deliver at 8 a.m. Tuesday, but this week you can't take delivery until noon Thursday. That's Thursday the 14th, right?"

• **Reassure the** customer that you can solve a problem as soon as you get more information. Explain how that process works and how long it will take.

• **Use positive** rather than negative words. *Example:* Don't say, "We can't have that *until* next Thursday." Say, "We'll have it *by* next Thursday."

• **Express an** understanding of the speaker's feelings.

• **Ask the** customer to continue to say more, if you're having trouble following the complaint. This allows the customer to offer new information without feeling as if previous information is being repeated. *Example:* "Can you give me an example of how the product performs differently now than when you first got it?"

Handling Angry Customers

Handling an angry customer is a real challenge. It can spoil your whole day. To keep that from happening, try to:

• **Keep smiling** and remain pleasant, no matter how nasty the customer gets. Remember that upset people are not attacking you personally.

• **Don't interrupt,** even to correct. Continue to listen. This can get rid of some of the emotional energy brought to the problem.

• **Ignore the** customer's style of delivery and personality. Don't let them distract you from listening to what is being said. Handle the problem with a calm, rational, "Let's solve this problem" approach. When treated this way, the customer usually will leave with better feelings about you and the company.

© Briefings Publishing Group, a Division of Douglas Publications LLC
2807 North Parham Road, Suite 200, Richmond, VA 23294
(800)722-9221 • (703)518-2343 outside the U.S.
Fax: (703)684-2136

• **Use language** the angry customer can relate to. Avoid jargon and technical terms that only you and the people you work with understand. Long-winded answers can increase hostility. *Example:* Tell the customer, "You'll get a corrected bill by the first of the month." Don't annoy by saying, "We will have to enter a revised statement into our computer database to modify your bill."

• **Don't keep** rehashing a negative encounter with your co-workers or in your own mind. Recounting the experience with others probably won't make their day any better — and rehashing it to yourself will just upset you. However, you may want to ask others how they would have handled the situation.

Get the Facts

To be effective, you must fully understand what the customer is saying before you can act. *You should:*

• **Find out** if the complaint is based on real happenings or comes from the customer's perception of things. *Example:* A customer is upset because his bill is much higher than his friend's. After calmly asking the customer a few questions and checking the records, you find out that his friend didn't request all the services the customer asked for. Explain, in a way that teaches rather than makes him feel stupid, that his bill is higher because he gets more services.

• **Openly admit** the mistake when a complaint is legitimate and assure that it won't be repeated, if possible. Thank the customer for bringing the problem to your attention.

• **Assure the** customer that you'll deal with the problem promptly. Give the customer a time by which you'll be back in touch with an answer. Then make sure you follow up when promised, even if it's only to tell the customer that you are still working to correct the problem.

• **Contact the** customer immediately once you have the answer. Conclude your conversation on a pleasant note by thanking the customer for alerting you to the problem. If you think that other customers may have the same problem, tell a supervisor or someone who can correct the matter before it prompts more complaints.

© Briefings Publishing Group, a Division of Douglas Publications LLC
2807 North Parham Road, Suite 200, Richmond, VA 23294
(800)722-9221 • (703)518-2343 outside the U.S.
Fax: (703)684-2136

MAKING THE TELEPHONE WORK FOR YOU

The telephone keeps us in touch with clients, customers, vendors and others.

The hints and tips here will help you be more productive, do a better job and, maybe, suffer a little less when all those calls start coming in at once.

Saving Phone Time

If you try to make 30 calls a day, fewer than eight are successful connections on the first try, according to AT&T.

George R. Walther, author of *Phone Power: How To Make The Telephone Your Most Profitable Business Tool,* suggests:

• **Scheduling calls** much like you would schedule in-person appointments.

• **Never leaving** messages, such as "just tell him I called" or "have her call me back later." Always leave a specific time when you'd like a call returned or when you'll call back.

Tag, You're It

Here's how you can end the "I'm returning her call, returning my call, returning her call from yesterday" routine.

• **Try returning** phone calls about 10 minutes before noon and 10 minutes before 5 p.m. Most people are in their offices at those times.

• **When people** you call aren't in, ask what is the best time to reach them.

• **Don't just** leave a message when someone isn't available. See if someone else can help you.

• **If you** do leave a message, make it clear when you will be available. If you're going to be away from your phone for the next few hours, make sure that's included with the message.

• **If you** just need some information, leave a message that suggests what to do if you're not in when they call back. Say something like, "If I'm not in, tell Pat to leave the figures with Fran." And of course, let Fran know someone may be calling.

Hold Please

Never put a person on hold until you've asked permission to do so. And wait for an answer.

© Briefings Publishing Group, a Division of Douglas Publications LLC
2807 North Parham Road, Suite 200, Richmond, VA 23294
(800)722-9221 • (703)518-2343 outside the U.S.
Fax: (703)684-2136

People will hold longer if they know the name of the person they're holding for. You might say, "May I put you on hold, so I can have Mary Smith in accounting come on to answer your question?"

But beware of the irate phone caller. That person will stay on hold for a very long time — getting angrier with each passing second.

Grrrrrrrrrrowlllll

Complaining callers deserve special treatment.

• **Irate callers** need to be handled promptly. If they aren't, their anger will grow. And they'll begin sharing their bad experience with others.

• **Tell angry** callers your name. Once people know your name, they'll get the feeling that someone is genuinely interested in helping them solve their problems. In fact, it's a good idea to have all people in your organization give their names when they answer their phones. It can be as simple as, "Maintenance Department, Joe speaking."

• **Don't transfer** angry callers just to get rid of them. If they have to be transferred to get their problems solved, tell callers the name and number of the person they're being transferred to. That way, if a call gets lost, the caller will know how to get back in touch.

• **When taking** a message from an irate caller, make sure the right person gets the message as soon as possible. Don't let the message get lost in a stack of other messages.

• **Before calling** back someone who has a complaint, make sure you and your voice are comfortable. You might want to make a couple of nonthreatening calls first to get your voice relaxed. It's a good idea also to have a list of points you want to make during the call to keep the conversation focused on solutions.

Bad Connections

Not all people call to complain. But even happy people will start complaining quickly if their calls aren't handled well.

• **Make sure** calls are answered right away. Business phones should be answered by the third or fourth ring. If people are "too busy" to promptly pick up ringing phones, then suggest some changes.

• **Answer the** phone clearly. In far too many cases, the person answering

© Briefings Publishing Group, a Division of Douglas Publications LLC
2807 North Parham Road, Suite 200, Richmond, VA 23294
(800)722-9221 • (703)518-2343 outside the U.S.
Fax: (703)684-2136

mangles the company name, slides over it, mumbles it or speaks so fast that the name is lost. Don't assume people know where they're calling. They may be returning a call and have only your phone number.

• **When taking** messages for someone who is not in, be careful about what you say. Comments — such as "She's on a coffee break" or "He's around here somewhere but I don't know where" or, even worse, "She never comes in this early" — create a bad impression. Explain simply that "She's not available now."

Your Three Minutes Are Up

Here are some time-saving phone tips:

• **When stuck** on the phone with a well-meaning caller, after the business conversation has come to an end, find a polite way to end the call. Say something like, "I just noticed it's 2:15 and I have a report due by 2:30" or "Just one more question before we hang up."

• **When calling** someone who will talk too much if allowed, begin the conversation with something like, "Hi, I have three questions for you."

• **If someone** asks to put you on hold, say "Fine, as long as you take down my number. I'm expecting a call and I may have to hang up." You'll be less likely to get lost on hold that way.

• **Consider using** a headset or shoulder rest if you spend a great deal of time on the phone. Your hands will be free to take notes or complete other tasks.

SHARPENING LISTENING SKILLS

Effective listening can make you more efficient and more productive. Unfortunately, most people are only 25 percent effective as listeners. The following tips and suggestions can help you become a better listener.

The Benefits of Listening

• **People will** respect and like you more because you have shown that you care about them and what they have to say.

• **You'll be** better informed, because when you actively listen, you learn more.

• **You'll be** better able to get things done, because you'll understand how to motivate people when you pay attention to what they're really saying — and thinking.

• **People will** listen to what you're saying, because they realize that you have made them feel important — and they will want to please you.

What Good Listeners Do

• **Look at** the person who's speaking.
• **Question the** speaker to clarify what's being said.
• **Repeat some** of the things the speaker says.
• **Don't rush** the speaker.
• **Pay close** attention to what the speaker is saying.
• **Don't interrupt** the speaker.
• **Don't change** the subject until the speaker has finished his or her thoughts.

How to Listen Better

Studies conducted at the former Sperry Corporation uncovered these keys to good listening:

• **Listen for** ideas, not just for facts. When you listen only for facts, you may not grasp the ideas or themes of the speaker. Here are some questions you might ask yourself when listening:
   —Why am I being told this information?
   —What does it lead to?
   —If that's true, what does it prove?

• **Judge what** the speaker says, not how it is said. Don't let the speaker's delivery get in the way of your understanding the message. Ignore any peculiar mannerisms or speaking problems the speaker may exhibit.

• **Be optimistic** when you listen. Try to find something of interest in the subject no matter how dry it may seem at first. Open your mind and try to find out what attracted the speaker to the subject.

• **Don't jump** to conclusions. Don't listen to the beginning of a sentence and try to fill in the rest. Wait and keep listening. Clear your head of your own ideas and listen to those of the speaker.

• **Be a** flexible listener when you're taking notes. Determine as soon as possible how the speaker puts forth his or her ideas, and gear your note-taking style to the speaker's style. *Example:* Ask yourself, "Is the speaker concise or does he or she take a while to make a point?"

• **Concentrate.** Remain relaxed but attentive. But don't become tense, or you'll make any distractions more pronounced. *Your best bet:* Try to remove as many distractions as possible. *One way:* When going to a meeting, get there early and sit up front where there will be fewer distractions.

• **Remember that** you can think at least four times as fast as someone can talk. This means that your thoughts will race ahead of the speaker's words — and you can become so detached that you'll have a hard time catching up with what was said. To stay on track, try to summarize what was said, or interpret the speaker's ideas, or evaluate the speaker's logic. You'll have time to do these things because your thoughts move so swiftly.

• **Work at** listening. Try to listen alertly and enthusiastically. Strive to "be alive." *How:* Respond to the speaker by giving feedback. *Examples:* Come up with an appropriate comment, smile if appropriate, summarize what the speaker just said.

• **Keep your** mind open — and restrain your emotions. Don't be distracted by strong words that may offend you. Train yourself to note the presence of emotional words — but to let them pass without an emotional reaction on your part. Work on interpreting and evaluating what the speaker is saying.

• **Practice mental** exercises. Use every opportunity to sharpen your listening skills. Work on your attitude. And practice, practice, practice.

A Few More Tips

Try these two valuable tips, which will help you develop rapport with the speaker. They were suggested by Joseph A. DeVito in *The Interpersonal Communication Book, Sixth Edition* (HarperCollins).

• **Accept the** speaker's feelings. Show that you have empathy for the person and his or her problems.

• **Ask questions** to let the speaker know you are paying attention to him or her. People realize you're listening to them when you ask a question, wait for an answer, and follow up with a related question.

AIM to Listen

Try this simple formula, from *The Secretary* magazine, that will help you remember three vital listening concepts. It's called AIM.

• **A — Attention.** Don't fake paying attention. If the person is important enough to listen to, then try to resist distractions.

• **I — Interest.** Try to maintain interest even if you don't think the topic or person is interesting. Tell yourself that the content might prove useful to you someday.

• **M — Motivation.** Try to motivate yourself by going over all the reasons you should pay attention. Be sure to list motives that offer you the greatest benefits.

WRITING EFFECTIVELY

To be a good writer, you must learn to focus on who your readers are — whether you're writing a memo, a letter or promotional material.

Write to them as you would speak to them — clearly, simply and cordially. Write to inform your audiences, not to impress them with your verbal acrobatics. They'll appreciate your straightforwardness and you'll save time and energy.

If you keep that approach in mind and use the tips and hints presented here, you'll tackle your writing tasks more easily and more effectively.

Getting Started

Whether it's a letter, report or memo, if it's worth writing, it's worth writing well. Don't set out to "dash off" something. Consider these guidelines:

• **Start with** a purpose. What is your message?

• **Organize.** Establish your ideas before writing. An outline can help you do this. Or simply make notes on the *who, what, why, where, when* and *how* of your message. You want to be brief and to the point, but you also want to be complete. You owe your reader all necessary information.

• **Make a** mental picture of your reader. If you don't know the reader, try to imagine what she or he is like. Or picture someone you know. Try to see your writing through your reader's eyes.

• **Write to** communicate and to get the desired reaction or response. Do not write to try to impress.

© Briefings Publishing Group, a Division of Douglas Publications LLC
2807 North Parham Road, Suite 200, Richmond, VA 23294
(800)722-9221 • (703)518-2343 outside the U.S.
Fax: (703)684-2136

• **Have a** conversation with your reader. Write in a way that comes naturally. Use words that come easily to mind. Don't worry about style. Style will emerge the more you write this way.

• **Use simple,** plain English. Write with nouns and strong verbs. Use short words. Lincoln used words of five letters or less for 70 percent of his Gettysburg Address.

Keep sentences to an average length of 17 words. Longer sentences discourage many readers. Make paragraphs no more than six lines long. Tight writing invites the reader to continue. Faced with long blocks of copy, most readers turn off.

• **Use specific** words. Avoid vague words that can be misunderstood. (Don't say "office equipment" if you mean a personal computer.) Anything you have to explain to yourself, you had better explain to the reader.

• **Be careful** with names, dates and numbers. Check everything. Don't expect someone else to pick up your mistakes.

Writer's Block

If you're still having trouble getting started:

• **Try reading** for a few minutes. Read examples of the same form of writing you're working on.

• **Start writing** what comes easiest to you. You can always come back and write the beginning after getting warmed up. Many writers find it useful to rewrite the beginning after finishing. Your opening sentences may be weak or require additions because of what is written later in the body of the piece.

• **Keep writing** something, strong or weak. You can always rewrite.

It's Written — Now What?

• **Revise, revise,** revise. Reduce, rearrange and rewrite to improve.

• **Look at** the major pieces of text. Do they all belong? Are they in the proper order?

• **Are there** paragraphs or sentences that don't add anything to your message?

• **Are there** words or phrases you don't need?

• **Are there** shorter words that would express the same thought better or just as well?

© Briefings Publishing Group, a Division of Douglas Publications LLC
2807 North Parham Road, Suite 200, Richmond, VA 23294
(800)722-9221 • (703)518-2343 outside the U.S.
Fax: (703)684-2136

• **Have you** got rhythm? As mentioned, a good writer aims for an average of 17 words per sentence. However, to communicate effectively, you should vary the length of your sentences. If your sentences and paragraphs vary little, work to change them.

• **If you** received the piece, would you read it? Does it have an attractive and readable look? If you see a great mass of gray type, think about breaking it up with paragraph headlines or with lists of material. Both make information easier to find.

• **Read it** out loud. You'll find out if your copy is conversational and natural. And, when copy is read aloud, mistakes are more obvious. Natural pauses appear. Places where punctuation is needed for proper understanding show clearly.

• **When you've** finished writing something important, put it aside. Let it sit for a day or two, if possible. You'll come back with a fresher point of view.

Proofread It

Once it's written, it must be carefully proofread. If this step isn't done well, the best writing suffers. To proofread more accurately:

• **Increase the** size of your proofing copy on your computer or copying machine. Mistakes show up more easily in larger print. Make sure any manuscript you'll have to proofread will be typed double-spaced.

• **Read once** to check spelling of proper names and accuracy of numbers.

• **Read again** to check subject-verb agreement.

• **Read backward** (from last word of sentence to first); this overcomes the tendency of speed readers to skip syllables and words.

• **Read syllable** by syllable — out loud.

• **Have at** least one more pair of eyes proof it.

More Tips

• **Accentuate the** positive. Research shows that it takes the mind longer to understand a negative statement than the same idea stated positively. *Example:* A reader can grasp "It succeeded" more quickly than "It did not fail."

• **Watch where** you place words such as *only* in a sentence; they can change your meaning. *Example:* "He *only* handed in one report." This implies that he may have done something else with a second report, or that he was the only one who turned in a report. "He handed in *only* one report," makes it clear.

• **Relying on** "very" isn't "very" good. Search for the word "very" in your copy and get rid of it by converting the adjective it modifies to a stronger adjective. *Example:* Instead of "very large," use "massive," or "huge." Instead of "very small," use "tiny," or "compact."

• **Eliminate useless** words. One study showed that the average business letter contained an average of 15 useless words. *Examples:* "please be advised," "we wish to draw attention" and "I have before me your letter."

• **Be aware** of two common problems: the misuse of "its" and "it's" and "your" and "you're."

You use "its" when you want to communicate possession. "It's" is a contraction for the words "it is." *Example:* "It's too soon to tell if its improved software will make a difference in sales."

"Your" also shows possession, as in "your" desk. And "you're" is a contraction of "you are."

• **Make sure** your nouns and pronouns agree. *Example:* It's wrong to say, "The group wants to reserve hotel space by Thursday for *their* June meeting." Use "its" with the singular "group."

• **Watch those** weasel words. Avoid using a string of words that creates the impression you're insecure or, worse yet, insincere. *Example:* "It *appears* that we *possibly may* be able to accommodate your request if we receive it by October 15." Even if you can't give a direct answer, try to be as frank and straightforward as you can. You'll appear more authoritative and credible to the reader. *Suggested rewrite:* "We'll try our best to accommodate your request if we receive it by October 15." Other weasel words to avoid overusing: "perhaps," "apparently," "seems," "generally."

• **Indent those** paragraphs. Although many secretarial schools still teach block style, research shows that indented paragraphs are easier to read.

• **Pretend your** next memo must be sent as a telegram that you have to pay for by the word. Make every word count.

• **Know how** long a memo should be: long enough to make the point and be clear to the reader.

• **Improve your** spelling. If you don't know how to look up a particular word, consult a dictionary or a thesaurus for a synonym. You'll probably find the word you can't spell.

• **Use nonsexist** language to avoid annoying other employees, clients or customers. *Example:* Use sales representative instead of salesman.

MAKING THE MOST OF MEETINGS

Too many meetings are poorly planned and poorly run.

The result: Time is wasted and money is lost.

Are you getting the most from meetings you organize or attend? Use the tips here to make sure you do.

Getting Organized

Any poorly planned meeting will be a time-wasting disaster. To keep this from happening, make sure you:

• **Schedule the** meeting at a convenient time and give all attendees adequate notice. Those attending should have enough time to do their own research on topics to be discussed and arrive prepared to intelligently discuss the meeting's topics.

• **Distribute an** agenda before the meeting and then stick to that agenda during the meeting. Side issues that may be raised before or during the meeting should be handled by individuals after the meeting or, if necessary, addressed at a follow-up meeting.

• **Give one** person responsibility for running the meeting. The meeting director doesn't necessarily have to be the top executive in the session. *Who works best:* Someone who can stick to the agenda, moderate the discussion, be aware of the time and move participants toward closure.

• **Make sure** the meeting leader establishes some brief but fair rules for the meeting. The lack of clear meeting rules is a major meeting time-waster. Attendees need guidance on how long they may speak or how long a discussion can last. If people know in advance that they'll have only so much time to make their points, they'll arrive prepared to be brief.

Important: Always ask yourself: Is this meeting really necessary? Cancel those sessions that really aren't. Ideal candidates for cancellation: regular weekly or monthly staff or department meetings — often held whether they're needed or not. Memos, reports, bulletin board notices or other communication techniques often can handle the routine announcement functions of such sessions — at a considerable savings of time and money.

Room for All

Perhaps the most-overlooked task in planning a good meeting is finding the right meeting room. *Some tips:*

• **Make sure** you pick a well-lighted room with no unnecessary distractions. *Also important:* adequate and comfortable seating, with room for easy note-taking by those attending.

Remember: Maintain a comfortable room temperature. If it's too warm, attendees will grow sleepy. If it's too cold, they'll be too uncomfortable to concentrate well.

• **Keep refreshments** light. Have plenty of ice water. Fruit is a good alternative to heavy pastries or cookies.

• **Make sure** the room is equipped with all the necessary tools. *Examples:* an overhead projector, TV and VCR. *Tip:* Use a chalkboard or flipchart to write down ideas. Participants will be able to keep track of what ideas have already been mentioned.

• **Pick a** productive time of day for your sessions. Early afternoon meetings tend to bog down, especially when participants arrive after eating a heavy noontime meal. *Tip:* Schedule frequent breaks — and encourage participants to get up and walk around during breaks.

Inviting the Right People

• **Invite only** those who have direct responsibility for the items or actions to be discussed at the meeting.

• **If you're** invited to a meeting that you're not sure you need to attend, ask the meeting planner to explain why you're the best person to attend. *Idea:* Suggest another person to attend if you feel he or she is more appropriate.

• **Keep the** number of persons in your meeting at a minimum. Six to eight participants is an ideal number.

Remember: The more people in your meeting, the more difficult it will be to communicate effectively. *Tip:* Use follow-up meeting notes or individual

© Briefings Publishing Group, a Division of Douglas Publications LLC
2807 North Parham Road, Suite 200, Richmond, VA 23294
(800)722-9221 • (703)518-2343 outside the U.S.
Fax: (703)684-2136

department meetings to relay discussions or actions taken at the main meeting when you believe a larger group needs to be informed of what has been discussed.

• **Understand that** meetings mean more to some people than places to consider new ideas and take action. Meetings, for some, are a great place to boost egos and demonstrate one's importance to the organization.

How to handle egos: Suggest that the meeting leader adequately introduce those attending or speaking at a meeting. When the leader makes appropriate introductions, individual ego-boosting needs can be taken care of at the start. Those attending can then spend less time telling the group why they are so important to the meeting and more time discussing the topics at hand.

Discussion tip: Consider asking senior managers to hold off making comments until late in meeting discussions. *Why:* Junior staff members may be intimidated by comments made earlier by managers — and might be less likely to share their ideas.

Important: Make it clear that performance in your meetings isn't judged on specific speeches or witty remarks made by individuals during the course of the meeting. Meeting performance is judged on how well the group addresses the issues being studied and discussed.

Putting people in the right seats can also affect how well a meeting runs.

If you want to spark a confrontation, seat opposing people across from each other at a table, so they're facing one another. If you want to avoid a confrontation, seat opposing parties next to each other. Confronting someone is more difficult when seated side-by-side.

If one person is likely to interrupt the meeting with personal complaints or concerns, seat that person to the side of the meeting leader. *Reason:* This arrangement reduces the amount of eye contact between the two and cuts down on opportunities to interrupt.

Setting a Target

Every meeting you attend should have a specific objective. Rather than "boosting profits," a successful meeting might set out to find "three areas where we can cut production costs in an effort to boost profits."

Tip: Don't be bashful about tactfully asking what a meeting's objective is.

© Briefings Publishing Group, a Division of Douglas Publications LLC
2807 North Parham Road, Suite 200, Richmond, VA 23294
(800)722-9221 • (703)518-2343 outside the U.S.
Fax: (703)684-2136

Getting Started

People appreciate promptness and succinctness. If you're running a meeting, start it on time. Latecomers may be embarrassed the first time they arrive — and the meeting is under way. But after a few prompt starts, they'll get the idea that your meetings start on time.

If you're attending a meeting, always arrive on time.

Tip: Set specific time limits for meetings. Don't just schedule a specific starting time. Set a closing time as well. Let all know up-front that they have a specific amount of time to accomplish what's on the agenda.

Additional tips:

• **Try to** begin and end each meeting on a positive point that brings the group together. This technique helps to build an atmosphere of teamwork.

• **If you're** invited to a meeting with no scheduled finish time, ask beforehand when the meeting leader thinks the meeting will wrap up. This will help you to schedule the rest of your day. Schedule meetings with odd start times   10:06 a.m., for instance — to help reinforce that a meeting will begin promptly at a specific time.

Coming to Order

Even if the meeting you're attending isn't covering the most exciting topics in the world, there are a number of things you can do to make sure you're getting the most from what's being discussed. *For example:*

• **Make sure** you're an active listener throughout the meeting. Don't let yourself become preoccupied by thoughts of other urgent tasks you should be addressing.

• **Take good** notes. Don't depend only on formal meeting wrap-up notes or action lists to be compiled later by the meeting leader. Your notes may help you recall specific points that relate directly to your area of responsibility.

PRESENTING WITH POWER

The next time you're faced with giving a presentation, try these ideas to help you become more confident, authoritative and persuasive.

© Briefings Publishing Group, a Division of Douglas Publications LLC
2807 North Parham Road, Suite 200, Richmond, VA 23294
(800)722-9221 • (703)518-2343 outside the U.S.
Fax: (703)684-2136

Build Your Confidence

Good presenters are confident in their presentation abilities. And they're confident in their subject matter. *To boost your confidence:*

• **Do your** homework thoroughly. Learn all you can about the subject of your presentation.

• **Know your** audience. Learn how much the audience knows about your topic and which specific details the audience will be interested in.

• **Consider the** audience your ally. *Remember:* The audience wants you to succeed. Nothing would make your audience members happier than to go away with what they came for.

• **When asked** to speak, determine what the people who invited you expect. Ask them to complete this statement: "As a result of the presentation, we hope the audience will ..."

Avoid the Boring Trap

To be sure that your presentation doesn't fall into the boring category, use these techniques:

• **Use your** leg muscles to get out of the chair after you've been introduced. This will prevent you from slouching as you get up. *Result:* You'll appear more energetic.

• **Don't start** by apologizing for something. *Examples:* reminding the audience that the room is warm or that you're not an experienced public speaker. Apologies such as these may set a negative tone at the start of your presentation.

• **Smile as** you begin. People like to work with people who seem happy about what they're doing.

• **Be enthusiastic.** It's easier for people to listen to presenters who seem to care about what they're sharing.

• **Avoid reading** your presentation. Most audiences dislike being read to.

Preparing Your Presentation

When you prepare your presentation:

• **Try compiling** your research and information on index cards, on large Post-it Notes or on a computer. Don't worry at first about putting your information into categories.

© Briefings Publishing Group, a Division of Douglas Publications LLC
2807 North Parham Road, Suite 200, Richmond, VA 23294
(800)722-9221 • (703)518-2343 outside the U.S.
Fax: (703)684-2136

• **Next, see** if you can then put the information in categories. Some items will fit nicely; others won't. Don't worry about that at this stage.

• **Determine the** key points that you want to make. Then see if the categories you established cover those points.

• **Find a** way to work in any especially good information that doesn't fit into the other categories.

• **Put extra** emphasis on the beginning of the presentation. *Reason:* Either you grab the audience or you don't. And you must.

You might want to start with a strong statement that will capture the audience's attention.

You might want to use a story that relates to the audience and to the topic.

Or you might want to instantly communicate that you have a lot to say and not much time to say it by getting right to the point. *Tip:* Don't start with a story that is not related to your point. If the story misses, you're off to a bad start.

• **Prepare three** different presentations — one for the time you've been assigned, one for about 20 percent longer and another about 20 percent shorter. *Why:* Frequently you'll be asked to shorten your presentation because others ran long. Occasionally you may be asked to lengthen your presentation for some reason.

How to prepare: Prepare cards 1, 1A and 1B; 2, 2A, 2B, etc. If you're going to be speaking as planned, use cards 1, 1A, 2, 2A, etc. If you need to stretch the presentation, you can add the B cards; if you're going to shorten the presentation, use only cards 1, 2, etc.

• **Use short** sentences. Don't be afraid to use sentence fragments (sentences that don't contain a subject and verb).

• **Use comfortable** words that are easy on the audience. *Example:* Choose "use" instead of "utilize," "try" instead of "endeavor." *Remember:* You're not out to impress people with your vocabulary. You're trying to communicate with them. *Also:* Avoid any jargon or technical terms — unless all of the audience will know and expect them.

• **Put extra** attention on the conclusion of your presentation. Decide what you want to happen as a result of the presentation.

Examples: Don't just end the presentation. If you want to move the audience to some kind of action, make sure you end with a challenge or a charge.

You might close with a question that prompts discussion with the audience.

© Briefings Publishing Group, a Division of Douglas Publications LLC
2807 North Parham Road, Suite 200, Richmond, VA 23294
(800)722-9221 • (703)518-2343 outside the U.S.
Fax: (703)684-2136

Or you might conclude with the main point that you made during the presentation.

Using Statistics

If you want to use statistics in your presentation, remember that the ear can't record a factual figure the way the eye can. You might want to consider these suggestions when sharing statistics with your audience:

• **Round off** numbers. Don't say: "8,128 students." Say: "more than 8,000 students."

• **Instead of** saying "78 percent," say "about 4 out of 5."

• **Use examples** that people will understand. Instead of saying "a national cost of $60 billion," make it "$240 for every man, woman and child in America." *Another example:* "We're spending more on pet food than we did on food programs for poor people last year."

Using Audiovisuals

Audiovisuals can be used effectively to reinforce key points or statistics.

But remember: Audiovisual aids are just that — aids. They should be used only to supplement the spoken message in any meeting. *Consider these suggestions:*

• **Avoid overly** complex charts and graphs. If they must be used, put them in a handout for attendees to study later.

• **Remember the** 4x4 rule for overheads and slides. Use no more than four lines with no more than four words to a line.

Some Other Tips

• **Make sure** people can hear you. *One way to be sure:* Simply ask if everyone can hear.

• **Don't keep** coins or keys in your pockets. They could make noise that will bother your audience.

• **If you're** going to provide handouts, let people know that at the beginning of the presentation so they don't take unnecessary notes. Be specific about what the handouts will contain, however.

• **Place your** name, address and phone number on handouts so people know how to get in touch with you.

• **Just as** you're about to begin your presentation, picture a jewel on your listeners' foreheads. You'll appear to be looking into their eyes.

• **Early in** the presentation, break away from the lectern and move closer to your audience. *Why:* You develop a better rapport with the audience.

• **If you** have something in common with your audience, share that and at least imply that you know the audience's specific needs and will be addressing them.

• **Number your** cards or pages. If you drop them, you'll be glad you did.

• **Place a** second copy of your notes or presentation somewhere you'll be able to find it easily in case the first one is mislaid. Not having to worry about this will relax you.

Handling Questions

During a question-and-answer session:

• **Repeat each** question so everyone in the audience hears it. *Why:* It's a common courtesy. *Also:* It buys you some time to think about your response. It also makes the questioner feel good.

• **Maintain eye** contact with everyone, not just with the questioner.

• **Offer succinct** answers. If someone needs more elaboration, ask him or her to meet with you after the presentation.

• **Don't debate** with people who ask questions. If someone disagrees, say something such as, "I appreciate your views."

• **Don't guess** if you don't know an answer. Explain that you'll check on the information and get back to that person.

MANAGING TIME

"If I just had more time," is everyone's wish. But there isn't any more time.

Think, then, of how to use time better, not how to get more. Here are some steps to control time.

Decide to Get Organized

• **Give yourself** a pep talk.

• **Tell everybody** you know that you're going to get organized. To avoid

© Briefings Publishing Group, a Division of Douglas Publications LLC
2807 North Parham Road, Suite 200, Richmond, VA 23294
(800)722-9221 • (703)518-2343 outside the U.S.
Fax: (703)684-2136

embarrassing yourself, you will then get organized.
- **Set a** starting date.
- **Think of** how much money you can save and how much stress you can avoid if you get organized.

Find Out How You Use Time Now
- **For three** or four days, keep track of what you do with your time.
- **Divide your** day into 15-minute blocks.
- **Record what** you did for each block.
- **Don't wait** until the end of the day to record it. Do it throughout the day.
- **List interruptions** and record who or what interrupted you.
- **Give each** activity a degree of importance; for example, A, B, C.
- **After three** or four days, analyze how you spent your time. Find out what you could have eliminated, what wasted your time, who interrupted you most, what you could have delegated, when you got to your most important task, how you spent the beginning of the day, and when you were the most and least productive.

Set Long- and Short-Term Goals
You have to know *where* you're going before you know *what* to do to get there. You waste time if you spend it on something that doesn't lead to a goal.
- **Write down** your professional goals for the year. These should dovetail with your company's goals.
- **Then list** your personal goals for the year. *Examples:* "To take five strokes off my golf game," "To lose 20 pounds," "To have the house painted and driveway coated," "To read more in my field," "To get in shape," etc.
- **Make short-term** goals based on your long-term goals.
- **From them,** set your goals for the week.

Schedule Your Time
- **Start with** the list of things you want to complete by Friday.
- **Start a** "To Do" list for each day of the week. Don't keep it in your head. Put it on paper. Again, list only things that lead to your goals.
- **Each morning,** refine your "To Do" list for that day. Prioritize your list of things to do for the day with an "A" for the most important ones, a "B" for

the next important and a "C" for the least important.

• **Prioritize your** A's as A1, A2, A3, and so on. Finish A1 before moving to A2 and on through your A's. Do the same for your B's and C's.

• **Pick the** time of day you want to work on an activity. Allot so much time per activity. Try to complete each one in less time. You'll get more done this way.

• **Some thoughts** about your "To Do" list:

—Don't schedule every minute of the day.

—Schedule the most difficult task for your most productive time of the day.

—List the most unpleasant task as your first chore of the day. And do it first. It will occupy your mind if you put it off.

—Don't start with a lot of easy-to-do C's before getting to your A1. The day will be gone before you get to A1.

—If your A1 looks overpowering, break it into parts and work on them.

—Set aside some time to think and relax.

—Keep one "To Do" list, not a lot of scraps of paper.

How to Handle Interruptions

• **Intercept interrupters** before they get into your office. Talk to them as you slowly walk away from your office.

• **If they** want to meet, go to their office. You can leave when it's convenient.

• **Explain that** you're busy on a priority task. You'll give them time later.

• **Don't have** your desk visible through your office door. If they can't see you, they aren't tempted to interrupt you.

• **Have something** on each chair in your office so they can't sit anywhere.

• **Stand up** when they come in. Remain standing and glance at the clock.

Minimize Telephone Interruptions

If answering the telephone is not the major part of your job, here's how to use phone time to your advantage:

• **Do easy** jobs while on the phone — sign papers, read if you're waiting, or organize your desk and papers.

• **Develop a** plan for screening and delegating calls. Train people how to answer the phone.

• **Don't interrupt** someone else with an unimportant phone call simply because you want to talk.

© Briefings Publishing Group, a Division of Douglas Publications LLC
2807 North Parham Road, Suite 200, Richmond, VA 23294
(800)722-9221 • (703)518-2343 outside the U.S.
Fax: (703)684-2136

• **If you** can, establish times when you'll take phone calls.

• **Bunch your** return phone calls at a time you need a break.

• **Plan what** you're going to say if you'll be discussing complex matters. Jot down points to be covered. Thus you avoid having to make a second call to mention something you forgot.

If you're in a service organization where answering the phone is a major part of the job:

• **Analyze the** times when most calls come in.

• **Develop some** idea of trends.

• **Once you** find out when you get most calls daily and weekly, plan work for non-peak phone times.

Controlling Paperwork

The best way to control paperwork is not to let it get on your desk. Have someone screen your mail and organize how you'll handle what gets to you.

• **If possible,** handle a piece of paper only once. If you can't complete the action required, do at least part of it.

• **Read your** mail with a dictating machine or pad and pencil in hand. Answer as much of it as you can when you first pick it up.

• **Don't ask** for copies if you don't need them.

• **To avoid** amassing paper, store information on computer disks.

Other Time Management Tips

• **Ask yourself** these three questions: What are my co-workers and I doing that doesn't need to be done? Does anyone really need to do these things? What am I doing that others can do?

• **Use waiting** time to read, plan, study, review or write.

• **Do something** while watching TV. Sort papers, for example.

• **Isolate yourself** when you have to complete a major task.

• **Use travel** time to plan, listen, read, think or write.

• **Redesign forms** that take too long to complete. Ask this question: Is anyone using all the information provided? You can streamline most forms and eliminate some.

• **When you** want to end a meeting or leave an appointment without making excuses, wear an alarm wristwatch. *Also:* Use the watch to allocate a fixed number of minutes for office appointments.

• **Ask employees** for ideas on how to spend time more wisely. Find out what procedures can be combined, changed or eliminated to increase productivity.

• **Communicate to** every employee what five minutes of wasted time means on a company-wide yearly scale. Relate those numbers to profits and salaries.

• **Take a** hard look at those periodic reports to see if they can be written less often. Consider preparing reports every other month instead of monthly.

• **Include your** phone number on all correspondence. This encourages people to communicate quickly with an idea or concern.

• **If you** make an appointment well in advance, call the day before the appointment and remind the other person of it.

• **Send agendas** before meetings. Attendees won't have to take meeting time to collect their thoughts on the topics.

INCREASING PRODUCTIVITY

Your ideas and energy give life to your organization and enable it to function at its best. The more you realize your potential, the more you and your firm benefit.

You Can Get Satisfaction

To perform at your best and with more ease, you must rid yourself of habits of procrastination, according to James Braham, writing in *Industry Week*. Here are some specifics Braham recommends:

• **Remember the** "Four D's." When handling paper, dump it, delegate it, delay it or do it. After you have delayed something, allow sufficient time to see if you need to act on that particular item. If not, toss it.

• **Don't gift-wrap** the garbage. It's not necessary to do insignificant tasks perfectly.

• **Stick to** a time limit on those jobs that you don't like to do.

• **Set a** date and time to start a particular job.

• **Focus on** the results that will come from your accomplishing the task that you have been putting off. Think less about what has to be done and more about what will result when you finish.

Other Helpful Approaches

Excessive stress can interfere with performance. You can minimize it if you:

• **Set your** own daily or weekly goals. You'll get a feeling of pride when you reach them. Just be sure the goals are realistic.

• **Ask the** right person if you're unsure about something to do at work. Winging it or getting an answer from someone who isn't responsible for a particular decision could get you in trouble and increase your stress level. Bosses prefer employees who ask questions in order to get the job done right.

• **Stop trying** to change your boss. To build a better relationship, change yourself. Many people underestimate the power they have to improve a situation by changing their behavior and their expectations of others.

• **Try these** two tips from Joy Ufema, writing in *Nursing Life:*

—On your way home from work, select a spot along the highway. In your imagination, dump each day's stresses at the same spot.

—Write down three positive things you can do for yourself in the next week. Then do them. You've got to take care of yourself and your stress before you can offer your best to the people you work for.

How to Work Better, Not Harder

Certain tasks tend to become routine. Try these tips and ideas to make your routine a lot smoother.

• **When photocopying** a long article or memo, start with the last page first. That way, when you're finished, both the original and copy will be in the correct page order.

• **To avoid** handing out an original as a copy — requiring that you later make copies of a copy — try this: Put a white self-adhesive label (the 3/4" dots work well) on the original. The dot won't show on the copies but will stand out on the original.

• **Consider enlarging** a newspaper clipping on the copying machine before circulating it in the office. The clip will be more eye-catching and quickly readable.

• **Get yourself** and those you work with a "Later, please" sign. *Reason:* It can easily be put on the door or on the desk to communicate to everyone that you don't want to be bothered at a particular time.

• **Develop binders** of commonly sought materials. This way, you will avoid sorting through files to retrieve the answers to frequently asked questions.

Make Computer-Use Easier

To avoid computer problems, take advantage of these tips:

• **If you're** working at a computer terminal and experiencing visual fatigue, blink more often. With each blink you lubricate your eyes.

• **Wipe your** computer screen with one of the many cleaning pads available for this purpose. You'll cut down on glare and eye strain.

• **You just** spent an hour racing a deadline to type a report into your computer. Zap! A power surge eats all your work. *How to protect yourself:* Buy an inexpensive windup cooking timer. Most have settings in 5-minute segments up to an hour.

Before you start to type, set the timer for 15 or 20 minutes, less if you like. When it buzzes, save the file and then start again.

Cost-Effective Phoning

• **Use toll-free** numbers whenever possible. Use toll-free information whenever possible. Call toll-free information (800-555-1212) to get numbers or buy a toll-free directory. Be sure toll-free numbers are recorded in office telephone files.

• **Circle or** highlight phone numbers the first time you look each number up in the telephone directory. You'll save time when again searching for the numbers.

• **If you're** trying to call a business number after hours and the switchboard is closed, try dialing a number or two higher. *Example:* Instead of dialing 555-1000, try 555-1001. *Reason:* You *may* be able to bypass the switchboard and find someone on a live extension.

• **Make sure** you have the correct pronunciation and spelling of the names of your most important clients and customers. Be aware especially of those that are hard to pronounce or spell. Also, don't assume that a particular name is male or female. Many names are used by both sexes.

• **Use telephone** message slips that have a line for the phonetic spelling of the caller's name. They can save you the embarrassment of mangling a

© Briefings Publishing Group, a Division of Douglas Publications LLC
2807 North Parham Road, Suite 200, Richmond, VA 23294
(800)722-9221 • (703)518-2343 outside the U.S.
Fax: (703)684-2136

caller's name during the return call. *Example:* You take a call from Ms. Shiloh. After writing down the correct spelling of her name, you also write down the pronunciation phonetically, *Shee-low.*

• **When using** a speaker phone, always ask the person on the other end if you can be heard clearly. Many speaker phones sound hollow, and some people don't like to deal with them.

• **Call instead** of writing a letter if it serves the purpose as well.

• **If you're** having trouble making contact with someone for the first time on the telephone, consider sending your message to her or his fax machine.

• **Put the** phone numbers for all emergency services on all phones.

• **Take a** look at your small memo pads to be sure that your phone number and extension, as well as the name of your company and its address, are included. These items save people time.

And remember to include your extension on interoffice correspondence as well. Co-workers will appreciate the time saved too.

Cost-Effective Mailing

• **If your** firm is overpaying postage by as little as $10 a day, the cost of an electronic scale can be offset in a few months. Suggest looking into the purchase of such a scale. Most units sell for between $750 and $1,000, but you can find less expensive ones that will do the job.

• **Use your** electronic postage scales to count large numbers of identical booklets or brochures. The simple math in weighing a few brochures and then multiplying can save lots of time over hand-counting individual items.

• **Try sending** meeting and appointment reminders on a post card. *Reasons:* It saves on postage, grabs attention and can easily be paper-clipped to appointment calendars.

• **When mailing** something important, such as invitations to a key event, include yourself in the mailing. This is one way to make sure the items made it through the post office and into the right hands.

• **Use the** lowest class of mail service that will get the required job done. Not all mail should be sent out first class.

© Briefings Publishing Group, a Division of Douglas Publications LLC
2807 North Parham Road, Suite 200, Richmond, VA 23294
(800)722-9221 • (703)518-2343 outside the U.S.
Fax: (703)684-2136